Violets
in the
Snow

To Zilole
With Love
a taste of dreams!
Edyth
Christmas 2001

Violets
in the
Snow

Poems by
Joy MacArthur

Printed by 637997 Ontario Limited
Windsor, Ontario
Setup and Design by Rick MacArthur
Cover Photos by Dan Reaume

ISBN 0-9689349-0-0

This Book is Dedicated to

My Son Rick

whose help and encouragement gave me the courage to risk.

Contents

Risk

To laugh is to risk appearing the fool.
To weep is to risk appearing sentimental.
To reach out for another is to risk involvement.
To expose feelings is to risk exposing your
true self.
To place your ideas and your dreams
before the crowd is to risk their loss.
To live is to risk dying.
To hope is to risk despair.
To try is to risk failure.
But risk must be taken because the greatest
hazard in life is to risk nothing.
The person who risks nothing; does nothing;
has nothing and is nothing.
One may avoid suffering and sorrow but simply
cannot learn, feel, change, grow, love, live.
Chained to certitudes the individual is a slave
and forfeits freedom.
Only a person who risks is free!

anon

Why I Write

Writing is a little bit like sharing
a dream. It mirrors part of who
we are and who we may
someday become. My reason
for writing is two fold: First for
personal fulfillment, and second
in the hope that something in
these words may touch a
reader's heart. That is enough!

Acknowledgments

Sincere thanks to my husband Richard for his patience and understanding during the many hours that I spent compiling this book.

My gratitude to my children Darlyn, Christopher and Timothy for their listening to my poems over and over.

Very special thanks to son Rick without whose support and business expertise, editing, layout and design this book would not have come into existence. Rick I can never thank you enough.

Hats off to Irv Barat who thought he retired from teaching at St. Clair College only to begin sharing his poetry talents with those of us continuing to learn in retirement. Thanks Irv.

Laurie Smith from the Arts Council of Windsor for her dedication to the art of prose and poetry among her other tasks. Laurie your knowledge and guidance has helped us polish and fine tune our work in preparation for publication. Thanks.

Thanks to all my friends at Wink, whose comments and suggestions have helped me tremendously. Also The Live Poet's Society and The Writer's Group of Windsor and Essex County. Your encouragement has lifted me high enough to risk.

Nature
Spiritual

(I will lift up mine eyes unto the hills…Psalm 121)

Rainbow Mountains

In the 'rose red city' of Petra half as old as time,
sits a gem above the desert of Wadi Mousa.
The rocks on the mountain face twinkle above
salmon and pink speckled sand.

The sun spills over craggy peaks, splashing
down the sides, like rushing water
falling over steep jagged walls, anxious
to meet the crystals on the coral floor.

Like a fiery sword, the sun bounces and
romps in the shade's teasing light.
Delicate hues of mauve, rose and lilac
slide into tones of grey, green and blue.

Petra sits like a diamond in a ring of mountains,
at the end of the siq's towering walls and long
winding path cut through solid rock leading to
the Treasury, and Aaron's high, holy sanctuary.

As I leave this range of Rainbow Mountains;
This place of sacred monasteries, tombs and
temples, with treasures from ages past.
"I will lift up mine eyes unto the hills"…

("The setting sun sets fire to the hilltops
... "Sirach 42)

Beauty of the Night

A silvery light skips
 across rippled water.
The sun sinks
 beneath a salmon sky
A ball of orange flame
...."Sets fire to the hilltops".

Lovers lounge on
 blanket of cool sand.
Chills slither up their spines
 pulling oversize tops down
 to hug bodies tight.

They watch.
Wait.
Whisper low.
The sun bows
 then dies.
The curtain falls on close of day.

The restless wind weaves
  eerie shadows
    floating down
      on film of steel grey mist,
        creeping, curling, closing in,
        on beauty of the night.

Stars appear...
  one, two and more.
    pour down
      like a sudden summer rain.
Sparkling diamonds
  glisten like sunshine
    kissing snow.

Abraham's descendants
  dot black velvet dome.
Mother moon round and full,
  journey's high,
    looks down
On the beauty of the night.

(Our bones are dry, our hope has gone;
we are done for Ezekiel 37:5-11)

Miracle of the Dancing Bones

She wanted to dance.
Kick up her heels, balance
    on the balls of her feet.
Slide across smooth, slippery
    ballroom floors.
To be lifted up by the music,
    let the tempo lead her;
        the rhythm move her,
            feel the vibration sink
                deep into her weary bones.
Her brittle, dead, dry bones.

She felt spent, arid drained of
    spirit.
Heavy, depressed like brittle,
    dead, dry bones.

Suddenly a vision appeared.
She saw a mound resembling
    a sand castle but it was a pile
        of human bones.
Brittle, dead, dry bones,
    lying still in death
        like those of "The Killing Fields."

She heard a rattling noise.
Saw bones move, join together
by sinew, muscle, flesh and skin,
but there was no breath,
no life…

She heard a voice coming from
the four winds…Spirit's breath
entered them;…breathed life
into the brittle, dead, dry bones.

They stood up and began to dance,
like fairies sighted on a green
velvet lawn on a misty morning.
They wore chiffon gowns in pastel
shades, flowing and swaying
in rhythmic symmetry.

She rose to her feet and joined
the other once brittle, dead, dry
bones, lying in the valley.
And they danced.

Aurora Borealis

Once I saw a luminous lights glow in the north west sky.
Watched it journey across the firmament like chariots of fire.
Thrilled as it set the sky ablaze in tongues of light.
And marvelled at the awesome beauty of the north.

Iridescent ribbons trailed leisurely like reams of ticker tape
    streaming down on a hero in a welcoming parade.
I stood spellbound as arches formed rose up,
    radiated rays to the height of heaven's door
    before plummeting down in waves and curls.

I wondered as new storms leapt higher, forming panels
    flowing like transparent draperies caught in a gust of wind.
Then suddenly exploding in space like a rocket blasting
    off at Cape Kennedy.

Now, I thirst for those spiraling lights that climb
    to the limit of the apex and touch greater,
    more thrilling altitudes before falling again,
    pouring a hailstorm of particles spewing into the
    atmosphere as bands disperse.
Who can say there is no God?

Winter's Rainbow

Winter's Rainbow is music,
  is myth, is mystery, is superstition
  and is poetry.
It inspires artists, stimulates the imagination,
  summons the Muses.

You can feel its rhythm in your bones
  as it leaps to a higher crest
    then suddenly sinks into deep valleys
      only to begin all over again.

The extravaganza acts out its drama
  in the dark sky in iridescent flickering
    patterns of dappled light, drifting up,
      dipping down then fading into oblivion.

Winter's Rainbow rises like a jet plane
  brushes angels' wings, before
    plunging to earth like a falling star.

Shooting a tunnel of light higher and higher
  spraying rays of diffusive radiance into
    fire crackers rising brightly then crashing.

A sheer fabric unfolds into bolts of flowing
  delicate veils, sprinkling and weaving
    pale threads that curve into rainbow colours.

Sparkling fountains of light, roll and spin
  particles that stucco the frigid sky.
Nature's light show comes out to play
  when the temperature dips to
    minus 40 degrees.

Violets in the Snow

Why do violets blossom in the snow?
Before March winds begin to blow.
They leap ahead of daffodils and tulips too.
Wave tasseled heads, of deep-purple blue.

Spindly stems break threw hardened soil.
In a modest way, they almost look royal.
Before other flowers awaken from below.
Violets like fairies dance in the snow.

Romp and toss all about in play.
Swish and flutter a cheery "hello".
Bud and bloom in a field of snow.
Bob like periscopes on a choppy sea.

Violets rush to greet us
When spring knocks on the door.
Splash mountainsides with brightness,
Near hills, rocks and trees galore.

Just wild flowers, some might say.
Quiet, modest, virtuous and gay.
Such ordinary shades of blue,
Make spring's promises come true.

They burst threw soil with tiny heads.
Without the bother of flowerbeds.
Violets sprout new life each year.
Bloom and grow in a garden of snow.

Special Events

Lady Love

Why can't a man say, " I love you?"
"She knows." He replies.
"I work hard. Buy things."
    She wants love.
If she can't have love,
    she'll take things.

A woman, who is loved, knows it.
So does everyone she meets.
There's a bounce in her step.
She seems to float above ground.

A hug …not too hard and,
" I love you." whispered
    in her ear,
        can make her deliciously
        happy.
A love note lying on the
    kitchen table can
        send shivers up her
        spine.

Fancy cards are nice.
Flowers and chocolates
    are lovely.
Elegant black lace night gowns
    are enchanting.
But secretly what every woman
    really wants to hear:
Three times a day, three
    hundred and sixty-
        five days a year is.
    " I LOVE YOU!"

P.S.
Now that the word's out
"Tell all the men."

The Lore of Love

Cupid's tensing his magic bow.
His passion tipped arrows ready to go.
A heart shaped box trimmed with dainty lace,
Is bound to bring a smile to milady's face.

Chocolate-coated candies will melt in her mouth,
And that's what Valentine's Day is about.
Romantic cards speak of love in bloom.
Imps spray potion darts and lovers swoon.

Dreamy eyed lovers toast with champagne.
Chubby cheek cherubs hum sweet refrain.
Seated in a secluded corner of the room.
Flickering candlelight enchants them soon.

Love rules the day when St. Valentine's king.
Sweet looking Cupids with arrows that sting.
A bouquet of red roses, a sprig of baby's breath.
Can anyone resist Cupid's amorous request?

My Irish Father

Above the mantle, memories
   cling to the violin you played.
It hangs on the wall like a
   crucifix as a symbol of your
     love and faith.
Your Irish spirit flowed over a life-
      time like blood through veins.
The violin evokes an image of you
   as I press its cool body to my cheek
     I feel your presence.
See your plump red cheeks bursting
   with vitality and health,
     lighting up the room with your smile.
I look at the tarnished green pennies
   you wedged under the balsa-wood
     bridge: "For better tone" you said.
It brings a tear and a smile to my face.
I recall how you rubbed rosin over the bow
   before drawing it over the strings
     to tune it up.

The irresistible rhythm of
  the music sets my toes tapping,
    echoing back on hardwood floors.
Uncle John on the pipes conjuring
  up that terrible Irish melancholy
    as we bid "Danny Boy "a last farewell.

Though you're gone Dad, your
  memory lives on in the music,
    in the stories and in the songs.
Especially on St. Patrick's Day
  when we're celebrating,
    "The Wear'in of the Green."

We gather around the room
  arms flung across shoulders
    clowning, dancing, laughing
      and crying.
Dad, your Irish spirit lives.

An Irish Story

St. Patrick's Day
Gathering of clans
Celebrating Irish history
A green hue veils the universe

Melodious orators
Poetic tales
Weaving a tapestry
On background of rolling
Green hills
Transcending
Generations of time

Through the medium
Of music, story and song
Oral tradition alive in Ireland

Between verses
Fiddlers romanticize
Legendary tales
Immortalize Irish heroes
Twinkling blue-green eyes
Mischievous grins
Drum rolls and pipes
Captivating rhythms

Soft shoed Kerry dancers
Leaping high like winged fairies
Spinning magic spells
St. Patrick
Holding high the Pascal candle
On Sleigo Hill
Converting Celtic tribesmen
To Christianity

Seasons

The First Season

When winter sheds his dark grey cloak
And the cold wind ceases to blow,
It's time once again to welcome spring,
Bidding tiny buds to open and bloom.

Blue-birds serenade on love's sweet song.
Red robins, chirp for an April rain.
Sailing, gliding across a blue sky,
Ushering the season with melodious strain.

Saffron crocuses poke heads above soil,
Splashing a shower of colour about.
Canary yellow clusters of daffodils rise,
To bask in the glow of warm spring air.

Tulips standing tall atop rolling green berm,
Don deep purple robes with pointed crowns.
Scarlet gowned maidens line up in a row,
Enchant anew and charm the eye
Of lovers strolling dreamily by.

Soft pussy-willows lie contentedly on limb,
Tucked in their plush grey huts,
Unfurling an array of fresh green curls,
Breaking forth into jagged new leaves.

All seasons are glorious each in its own way.
But the number one you'll surely agree,
Is that wand of magic that changes
Old things into new,
Transforming nature into resurrected bloom.

The Second Season

Summer time is the season I long to see
children laughing and shouting with glee,
swinging like monkeys from the big maple tree;
lounge on blankets spread over the lawn
see imaginary pictures in the sky,
as cream puff clouds drift lazily by.
Singing songs, clapping hands,
telling tales
of far away lands.

Petunias are spreading
their sweet scent about.
Gladiolas climbing long stems to bloom
to decorate tables and brighten a room.
Swimming and cottages
white sandy shores, sailboats and
freighters passing through
as we lounge on a park bench
enjoying the view.

Long summer days
windows open wide.
Fresh scented laundry snaps like a whip
blowing in the breeze.
Butterflies flit in the garden sunlight.
Cardinals and robins
sing far into the night.

I love summer, each passing day
and welcome
autumn when its day is due.
Each season has a purpose that is true,
but to choose one over another
I cannot do.

The Third Season

As we bid August a fond farewell,
And welcome autumn's magic spell.
Wine and topaz salvia bow in the breeze
Like graceful ballerinas dancing with ease.

Marigolds that bloom late summer and fall
Stand like strong soldiers, straight and tall.
Warm afternoon sunshine and chilly nights
Flaunt variegated hues before winter bites.

Trees ablaze in crimson and gold
A profusion of colour begins to unfold.
Nature's artist paints a brilliant view
A silent story no word can give due.

A piercing blast from autumn's horn
Reaps a copious harvest on tables adorn.
Roasting fowl in country church hall
Bring hearty appetites to feast in the fall.

Crisp frosty mornings nip at your nose
Blushing cheeks like a pretty red rose.
Now is the time to bid autumn good-bye,
Welcome winter with a deep sigh.

Autumn was created for a special reason
No artist can capture this glorious season.
Conceived long ago in a far away land
With a gentle stroke of the Master's hand.

The Fourth Season

A season without snow would never suit me,
    with wilderness so near, and the land is free.
To slide down a hill in warm attire,
    come in from the cold
    and curl up by the fire.
Saturday night hockey games to see,
    now come to us live on TV.
Tim Horton's coffee to warm our insides
    and chase away cold besides.
Gone are the days when we kicked boards
    to keep feet warm so toes wouldn't freeze.
Pretty snow falling, one flake at a time sprinkling a
    layer of soft icing over the ground.
No snow on the mountains, lakes and trees,
    imagine how bland that would be.
Winter sports like: skiing, and skating to do, curling,
    snowboarding and tobogganing too.
I love the fourth season in our "Winter Wonderland"
    with fresh cold air, snow squalls and all.
Four seasons include winter Canadians know.
It's unthinkable to imagine a winter without snow.

(There is a land of the living and a land of the dead; and the bridge is love, the only survival, and the only meaning. Thornton Wilder)

The Fifth Season

There is a tunnel we long to pass through,
       to reach that mansion in the sky we hope to.
We begin on this journey light hearted and gay
       as the end seems so distant and far away.
When faced with departure of those we hold dear
       we are sometimes gripped by the jaws of fear.
But death is a passage to an unknown land
       where loved ones await us on the strand.
Like a journey through the channel of birth
       we must pass through the darkness to see the light.
To arrive at the place we all long to be
       where pain is only a forgotten word.
Only joy and elation we'll know with the Lord
       united with those who have left the shore
       to seek paradise found and blessings galore.
They'll be waiting to greet us at the gate
       to welcome us home in our transformed state.
Beyond that far horizon we shall never find
       till we reach the fifth season spanning time.

(A time to be born, and a time to die; a time to mourn...
Eccl:3-3&4b)

A Season in Time

A time to remember those called, one by one.
A time to honour those gone home.
A dome of sapphire-blue canopies the
        open air cathedral.
An October sun offers condolence.

A "Garden of Eden" lush and green with
        meandering pathways through miniature
                parks like: "St.Francis, Theresa and Anne."
Bouquets of gladiolus, roses, and mums almost
        conceal markers lying low to the ground.
Grass, newly mown, mixing with delicate hues of
        flora, perfume the air.

A warm blanket of peace wraps its mantle
        round me holding me in its folds, reminding
                me, this is holy ground.
Love eclipses the narrow gap, separating life
        and death, drawing me into the fullness
                of that mystery of communion.

Swans float gracefully on quiet mirrored pond.
A bronze statue of a "Resurrected Christ"
    with open arms depicts the theme.
Resurrection Mausoleum Chapel stands behind.

The hymns "He'll Raise you up on Eagle's Wings"
    "City of God" and an Italian tenor's rendition of
        "Ave Maria" echoes in the afternoon sunshine.

Amid a backdrop of whispering pines, and stately maples,
    a gentle breeze stirs, fanning mourners
        caressing faces and drying tears.

Cemetery Sunday, a day to remember....
    consoling words from "Isaiah, Paul" and
        "Matthew's version of the Sermon on the Mount"
            purges aching hearts.
The Bishop sums up with Jesus' own words...
    "I am the resurrection and the life!"

Sunrise Sunset

Soon, I'll quit playing dodge ball.
For now, I'll keep kicking.
Pastel shades pamper my
    white hair and pale skin tones.
        so I opt for a makeover.
A touch of peach here, a dab of
    bronze there and I look brand new.

Exercise primes tired blood
    flushes out plaque, builds new
        bones and stabilizes weight.
A healthy diet, a new wardrobe,
And good friends and I'm fine.

Occasionally the calendar mirrors
    my dreary feelings.
So I call a friend and meet for lunch.
Happiness returns and I'm full of joy.
I know that the August of my life,
    is leaning toward a winter sunset;
        but my dreams span all seven
        stripes of the rainbow.
Here I'm young again, run, jump
    and feel jubilant.

When my mother's reflection
    stares back at me in the mirror
        I smile and say "Thanks Mom,
        for a wonderful life."

Serious
Poems

Deadly Legacy

My ancestor's gave me
    a bitter pill to swallow.
They gifted me with a cursed future...
        crippling my mind with stupor and
            chaining me to a state innocence.
Holding me captive by the genes
    they passed on to me.
Institutionalized me like an animal.
    for my own safety.
A zombie stuck in perpetual
    confusion.
Branded by an iron fisted blow...
    by a twist of DNA.
Strapped like a saddle around
    my unsuspecting mind.
Unbidden, thrusting me back
    to infancy.
The flip side of modern technology
    that cracked the code...
Not the cure.
I sit in purgatory waiting...
For a miracle drug to appear in a
    sterile lab.
To cut me free from the defective
    monster gnawing away at
        my brain cells.
To halt the deadly legacy of
        Alzheimer's disease.

The Acorn

Knock down the scaffolding
   of dependence on others.
Hang with the ease of a monkey
   swinging by the tail on
     a bamboo tree.
Push off with gay abandon
   like a skydiver
     jumping from an airplane at
      five thousand feet.
Pull the ripcord,
   float through the cobwebs
     of self doubt.
Fall through space with the
   lightness of a feather.
Let the wind
   lick your fears.
Let it crack the hard shell
   of pretense.
Let it rip out the rot.
Plunge deep into the pulp
   hidden beneath the layers
     of old wives tales.
Burrow through the lair of lies
   others told you
     and tear them out by the root.
Peel back the final layer
   of deceit and discover
     the mystery of the acorn.

Stuff of Dreams

Cut the ties...
There'd been quarrels.
You left. We refused
to agree. Come to terms.
Forgive. The plea. No
fault. There were good

times. Until our animal
appetites cracked the
surface of rational
thinking. Emotions
reigned as savage
rage ruled over fragile
psyches.

Insults hurled across
sacred barriers. Trust
crumbled like pottery
crashing on tile floor.
Cruel words cut the
tension of angry silence.

Sarcasm sliced thin,
splitting open old
wounds once healed.
Pain followed on the heels
of regret. Remorse
surfaced too late. The
flotsam of naked truth
floated on the wave of
a perfect dream.

Disconnected

Sitting by the window rocking, I gaze at the
clouds drifting lazily by, remembering...
times we imagined seeing lambs and
bunnies even angel faces as we lay on
our backs in the grass on summer days.

Now I see your face in the clouds.
Your eyes twinkling with mischief.
I hear you calling "Come on silly"
as we race through the willow trees
snatching leaves in our fists. Your
voice echoes. "Catch me if you can."

Then I realize it's only the wind whistling
through creaking branches of the
same willow trees we ran through so long ago.
The clouds always moving and changing forms
stimulating our childlike imagination.

How we cried when our dog Sandy was struck
and killed. The funeral procession a bunch
of neighbourhood kids, bawling and sniffling
unashamedly throwing a handful of soft earth
to keep him warm. Then dry branches atop to
keep him safe. Rolled a huge stone two
blocks to mark his grave.

You always beat me at checkers and rummy until
the day I caught you cheating. But I never
let on because, secretly, I wanted you to win.
I miss sharing childhood memories over coffee
with you and still would be happy if you won.

You had your faults, but your love and generosity
knocked them over like a
bowling ball striking ten pins.

I reach for the portable and punch those familiar
numbers. Then remember...
you can't be reached
by telephone.

Meditation on a Rose

Go out in early morning fair, when dew still
    clings to bush and leaf; before the sun sips
    moisture drop by drop; in the garden near
    the fence, lush with colour, find a rose.
Perhaps an apricot, deep pink or butter-cup
    yellow will be your choice...
Or yes, the American beauty, the loveliest of
    the lot.

Careful not to prick your finger on a thorn.
Take the scissors lying on the chair and snip
    about 12 inches from the top, then
    toss the cutters beneath the bush.
With the rag I gave you, swish the dampness
    dripping from the chair.
Then seat yourself comfortably upon it there.

Gently lay the rose upon your palm closing
    your eyes. Bring its sweetness to your
    nose to inhale its freshness.
Let the fragrance penetrate the mysteries of your
    whole, breathe in the aroma; let it sweep over
    your being.

Hold that scent, savour its essence. You may
    never know this sensation again.
As you feel it lying contentedly upon you palm,
    sense its weight, its coolness, its texture,
    lying tenderly there.
Stroke it gently, feel its softness, gently caress its
    delicate plush petals.

Notice the moisture, feel the air weaving between
    your fingers and become aware of touch in a
    new and sensitive light.
Let it flow over every fiber of your consciousness
    transcending all barriers and let it touch the
    centre of your deepest self.

Lift the rose to you cheek, yield to its feathery
    softness; let it seep into your flesh, bond
    with your body; feel it blend with you, comfort
    you and melt into you.

Raise it to you mouth, splash a hint of colour on your lips.
Remember the sweetness of a baby's tiny rosebud mouth
    and the hollow above, where the angel left its kiss;
    with the tip of your tongue taste the honey flavoured
    nectar bees love so well.

Stroke your eyelids, now blind from sight, and envision
    the picture once again.
Imprint that image on your sightless eye.
Recall its colour, texture, and focus upon your memory
    and snap the shutter with your inward eye.
Store it safely in the attic of your mind and stamp this
    memory firmly there.

Bring the rose to your ear and listen to it whisper to
your heart.
The rapture of love, the promise of fulfillment.
The hushed tones of a haunting lullaby...the giggling,
gurgling brook, frolicking and splashing by, the
quiet flow of water streaming its endless sigh,
telling tales of nostalgic days gone by.

Pull the pleasant aura into your ear and let it tap a
gentle beat.
Bask in its wonder, glory in its revelation; let it find
rest in the sanctuary of an intricate part of your
perception of beauty in the fullest sense.

Lower your rose to your lap, think about the language
it spoke to you. What did it say? How did it feel?
Was there a message, a meaning, a presence or an
awareness.
Did it whisper words of wisdom, brush your curiosity
and wonder?

Now open your eyes and take what it gave to you
freely, back to your noisy busy impersonal world;
because this feeling will never come again in quite
the same way.
But its reminisce will remain with you, long after the
rose has died and faded fast away.

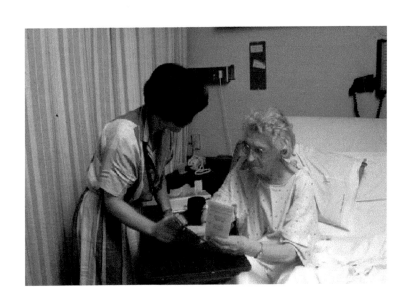

This Business of Dying

Who's afraid of dying?
It's harder to live.
Harder to lie here,
and know my pain
is burning a hole
in your soul. It's
your suffering, I
can't bear. The
way you have to
work at hiding
your emotions
behind the mask
of a half-smile.

Didn't I show
you how to wear
a "poker face?"
No, you're just
too honest to hide
behind the mask
of anything but
truth.

I've seen others die…
a little more each
day. The smell of
death hangs heavily
above the bed like
the sickening scent
of Easter lilies
filling a room. I wish
you wouldn't drag
yourself here each day
to try to make it easier
for me…to tell you:
"It's all right."

It's hard to let go,
when you keep
pulling me back,
trying to deny me
my reward. As if
saying good-bye
is any easier the
tenth time. But it
will get easier…
after…as the
months and seasons
fade like warm
summer days.

The time is not
our own to choose
but God's. I'll have
to wait my turn and
hold my tears tight
until I hear the
elevator doors
squeeze shut and
the motor hum.
Then I'll let the
tears sting my
cheeks; swallow the
lump in my throat.
You know me,
craving privacy,
needing my own
space.

I don't need a
miracle. I've spent
my time, both sensibly
and foolishly, all in
all received just
rewards.
I don't want to hang
around. I know
where I'm going.
All I want is to get
on with this business
of dying.

*(...Till we meet again, may God
hold you in the palm of His hand.
Irish Blessing.)*

Till We Meet Again

Seven years have passed
   and still I see your face
      transcending the years
         and miles with effortless grace.

Your hearty laughter rings
   through the dark hallways
      of endless space
        that separate us
           in time and place.

Then I remember,
   the promise we made
      "Till we meet again."
        And the tears fade.

Special People

Lost in Space

Walking in the garden,
  dry whiskered grass tickled my bare feet.
Sky grey, bloated like balloons ready to
  spill joy on a kid's birthday party.

You stooped to right a crooked swing,
  afraid the kids might trip, fall.
A steel brace sprang up, seized
  your shin, toppling you.

Hands clamped over my mouth.
Heart sinking like a stone in water.
A cold claw pinched my core.
Time stopped.
A bird chirped.
A breeze brushed my cheek.
The scent of sweet peas filled the air.
Dry mouthed. I asked.
"Are you all right?"
"I broke my arm."

"Dear God!" My mind a blank.
"Dear God, help me, remember."
Ashen you stood
   in the doorway, holding your arm.
"Ablana. Doctor Ablana."
You whispered leaning forward.

I find the number taped above. Spin the dial.
"Go to emergency."
Grabbing the tablecloth slipped your
   limp arm into its fold
      tied a reef knot at the base of your neck.

"In the car, Mom. Hospital."
Meekly you climbed into the front
   seat like a bewildered puppy.
I fastened belts.
Turned ignition.
Backed out.
Rain pellets peppered the windshield.
It didn't matter my spaceship had landed.

Mother Don't Smother

Mother why did you insist
   on colouring our grey world pink.
Read, "How to be a Jewish Mother"
   and practise on me.
Stuff me chockfull of chicken
   soup the first sign of a cold.
Caution me with too many "shoulds"
Hurry off to "Shaheen's Dry Goods"
   to pick up a piece of print
   to sew up a new dress,
   I didn't need or want.
Mother, I know you loved me.
But love isn't measured by the yard.
It's not so much what you give a child;
But allowing them freedom to
   make choices.
Let them make mistakes
   fall jelly side down...
Even do without sometimes.

Why Daddy?

Why did you cushion me
    from the rough edges of life?
I wanted to fall,
    knock the skin off my knees,
        feel my own pain.

I never imagined what lurked
    beyond these velvety green walls.
That my vulnerability would be
    an invitation for opportunists.

I felt helpless and alone.
Smoldering coals simmered beneath
    the surface of my quiet existence
        erupting into a violent rage.

You failed to guide me on how to float
    down safely…land easy.
Explain the rules of survival
    in the harsh language of the street.
That waggling tongues would nip
    at the heels of my good name,
        when I turned around.
Or, I'd be swept to my knees in humiliation,
    by waves of indifference.
"Be a nice girl Jenny," you warned.
And I was.

But you didn't warn me
   of the debilitating cost.
My friends laughed at me.
I hear their snickering yet...
   reverberating,
      like the drone of a tennis ball
         hitting a wall, repeating, "nice girl."

"Take risks" you'd said.
And I did.
Like Christie the teacher in space,
I challenged the universe and it exploded.
My pride swallowed into a vacuum
   of atmospheric vapour.

Sky Islands

We touched each
    other you and I.
Through years of
    ups and downs
        learning skills,
            sharing dreams.

Soaring above
    clouds, floating on
        puffs of imaginary
            castles, living on
                sky islands,
                    knowing they'd
                        be swept away.

Jacobs ladder, my
    escape hatch, lifted
        me high where
            angels dwell
                wearing crooked smiles.

You waited quietly
to catch me when
my bubble burst,
pick up the pieces of my
broken shell
polish my
tarnished image.

Perched in a dreamer's
paradise, above you,
I was alone, lonely.
you reached up
to rescue me,
your love swept me
off my crystal tower.

Whisked me down
winding pathways of
rose-scented avenues.
A mystical island
unimaginable
in a world of
make-believe.

Remembering Grandma

Grandma, I'm gazing at the photo of you and
Mother leaning on the fence, knee deep in
snow. You're wearing your Persian Lamb
coat and hat with blue feathers.

You marvelled how "Northern Lights"
lit up the sky, in Kirkland Lake.
The cold rewarded us with frost nipped noses.

Brisk evening walks, dressed like snowmen,
knitted scarves twisted round faces, our
legs stiff. We waddled like penguins.

Inside we disrobed by the door.
Heading for the crackling wood fire as we
shivered like quivering puppies, rubbing
hands and hugging the heat.

We lazed round the red and white checked oil-
cloth on the kitchen table, sipping hot
brandy coloured Lipton's tea.

When you returned home I cried, afraid I'd
    never see you again...alive. I should have
    known better. Your vibrant spirit kept
    flowing like a fresh mountain stream.

At eighty, you fell and broke your hip.
    Doctors warned, you'd never walk again.
    You proved them wrong. Sawing the legs
    off a kitchen stool, attaching casters, had
    you gliding over floors like a clipper ship.

Your powerful voice, reverberated off the wall
    like a loud clap of thunder, when you sang:
    "The Old Rugged Cross" or "I'll take you
    Home Again Kathleen" with such intensity
    it would make an elephant weep.

Now, sitting in a quiet place, closing my eyes,
    I imagine you rocking little Mary to sleep.
    Hear you singing," Mivourning." My
    Heart swells. Life for you Grandma was
    sunshine yellow, where you blossomed
    and grew in a rose garden called,
    "Tralee" on a summer day in June.

Remember Me Gently

Remember me gently:
For having a sense of humour,
   and the ability to laugh at myself.
For weeping when a friend shares bad news.
For letting tears flow at sad movies.
Remembering birthdays and anniversaries.
Loving the colour peach
   and enjoying the game of Jeopardy.

Remember me gently:
When life gets tough
   and the outlook grim;
For the hope of seeing beyond
   the silky grey lining
     of dark clouds
       and visualizing
         pink and purple streaks
          of tomorrow's promise instead.

For opening the window of my soul
   by casting out negative thoughts,
      replacing them instead with positive imagery.

Remember me gently:
For being lucky enough to call a friend
   when most needed.
Being content to listen
   when someone needs an ear.
Being available for another
   at the most inconvenient times.
For giving to charity when
   I can least afford to.
Most of all for loving others
   when they are quite unlovable.

Friday's child is loving and giving

Friday's Child

You marched around like The Music Man
swinging a baton,
high stepping the children in rhythm to
"You're a Grand Old Flag"
as you threw yourself actively into every
Nursery Rhyme Song or Game of Tag and Hide and Seek.
Others fell under your magic spell
eager to follow your lead
like the swans strutting down Main Street
in Stratford, every spring.

Watching you with Michael,
eyes wide with wonder,
grin rolling across his face,
a sparkling bundle of vitality
anxious to pick up your queue
for a fun packed day.

You rolled in the snow, built forts and snowmen
with sticky snow.
Planted gardens
sprinkled water to make it grow and screamed in shock
as Michael turned the hose on you ...soaking you.
The fun you had raking leaves and jumping into them,
scattering,
beginning all over again.

Tied a roped tire to a maple tree branch
pushed the swing so high he squealed in delight.
Friday's child...
I'm glad you happen to be my daughter.

Travel

Beneath the Surface

Deep beneath
Sahara sand
entombed in rock,
Pharaohs' dominate.

Within the cave
a ramp slopes
down, into damp, musty air
where artifacts peer
hauntingly through glass windows.

Myriad pathways
of long dead
waft pervasive odours through mystic corridors
as mildewed air collides
with body heat.
A ghostly shiver slithers over me
in the silence.

Our guide, Terrack, rhymes off: names,
dates, places
of Pharaohs.

We are met by the sight
of an unborn Egyptian Queen's son
encased in glass.

Returning to the present
leaving the past
buried
beneath its monument,
we ponder the wonders
as we
lunch in an open-air,
thatched roof restaurant.
Water filled balloons dangle
from the rafters
to bewitch pesky insects
whose sting kills.

(Ankh: an ancient Egyptian Symbol of Life)

Ankh's Journey

Evening's curtain hurries down
to kiss the hem of the grey
shroud enveloping the ruins
in Pharaoh-land.
A blitz of light erupts, flooding
the sky as "The Sound and Light"
show at Karnak unfolds,
portraying Egypt's past.
An arch of colour
skips across the sky, as I catch
a glimpse of a silhouetted ruin
in the mirrored surface of the Nile.
Millennium years
B.C.
They came.
They reigned.
They prospered.
And died.
Leaving towering monuments,
obelisks and statues standing yet.

(Touring Egypt)

Stepping Back in Time

In a whirl of excitement
we push forward,
hastening toward an amphitheare
tripping and feeling our way over
chariot-wheeled ruts
teeter-tottering in gutters
under a black tented sky.
.

A sleeping "Cradle of Civilization"
awakens to voices telling tales
of old kingdoms
depicted in hieroglyphic
murals painted on cave walls.

Queen Hatshepsut's Temple
cut into rock
speaks of a tribute to her reign.

Flood-lights flash
and usher
us out
steering toward an uncharted future.

Winter Events

Winterlude

If you want to taste something
different and scrumptious,
drive to Ottawa during Winterlude
sit on a snow bank along the Rideau Canal,
lace up your skates.

Find a wooden shack perched along
the shore with grey smoke pouring
out the chimney and
a rip roaring jack-pine fire crackling
in the stove's belly inside.

Glide over to the open window,
order a delicious, piping hot,
"Beaver Tail"
and fried golden brown
sprinkled with cinnamon
and brown sugar
or topped with sweet tasting maple butter.

Grab a fistful of napkins to catch
dripping juices.
Clutch the flat pastry
with your mitts on while your toes
freeze and your ears go numb.

Prelude

The landscape beckoned him
as he peered down the slope
and pondered the risks.
Smooth, innocent, inviting...
deceptive.
Sharp rocks hidden under
film of snow jutted out
under white covers ready to
impale the unsuspecting.
Tree stumps were
snow-draped like covers
over discarded art.
The adventure demanded
daring skill.
A gnawing hunger for thrills.
Satiated only by conquest.

Vertiginous Bliss

He pushed off.
Speed increased with descent.
The slope changed to a
hard, fast, slick surface.
The hill became master.

His face gripped with fear,
as he flew over bumps,
swerved round curves,
skinned trees,
knees tucked tight
then crashed into a hail
of blinding snow that bit,
pinched, needled
his face.

The jump rocketed him
into space and he floated
like a glider plane hovering
in the wind.

A hard thump awakened him
from a dream-like trance
as he plowed apart loose snow
and skidded to a halt.

Watching Jennifer Skate

Today, I saw a peach swan floating
    on a table of glass.
Saw her glide on ice like a feather
    in the wind.
Felt the rapture of her spin in the
    titillating dizziness of a Whirling
        Dervish dancer.
Her chiffon gown billowed into ribbons
    streaming like the puffs of a sail.
Every jump smooth, natural, effortless.
She enchanted me with music of an
    Irish Symphony.
And fed my loneliness with the haunting
    echo of a hollow flute.
Her layback spins captured a current
    of air, drawing me into a swirling eddy
        of mystery with breathtaking stillness.
I heard ice slash under the hot steel of her
    flashing blades.
She sparkled like bubbles on pink champagne.
Watching Jennifer skate is the essence of
    beauty and perfection.
Reflecting a peach swan gliding on a glass pond.
    A "Swan Lake" performance on ice.

Ice Sculptures

Silent splendour
carved from bale
sized blocks
of solid ice
shaped, by deft hands
chiseled into replicas of
Arabian chargers
fringed mane whipped back
by strong winds at full gallop.
Buxom female busts
adorned ship bows,
polar bears glassy surface
shone above ermine snow,
cat whiskered walruses
depicted mammals
native to the north.

Perched stern end
in a birch bark canoe,
sporting a buck-skinned
jacket, beaver tailed hat,
Pierre Trudeau sat
paddle high, thirsty
to plunge the deep.

A kaleidoscope
of light created
joyous carnival
atmosphere for
mid February
fairyland getaway.

Wishing

When the wind howls
in violent fits of rage
and rain raps at my window
like a fist in hurried frustration
I jump up, open the curtain
to see if you've come back.
But it's only the gate rocking
back and forth,
rolling and knocking
against the fence post;
or the hollow rattling
of an empty garbage can
somersaulting across
the driveway.

I can't help think you
are trying to signal me,
let me know you're all right.
Since you left I wish I had
told you
how I really felt,
but pride pushed itself
between us
you are gone
and it's long past midnight.

On the
Lighter Side

Rainy Day Blessings

Hoarding books is my sin:
tomes are a writer's inspiration
unique imagination
compiled with much frustration.

I stalk bookstores
peer at window displays
once inside, I'm hooked.

Muse over titles
snake in and out of rows
up and down isles
like a hypnotized worm.

Evocative covers intrigue me,
bright coloured jackets delight.
I slide a book off the shelf
inhale the pungent odour
of printers ink...intoxicating.

I try to discipline myself
wait for anticipated satisfaction,
to savoir the flavour
enjoy later.

But it's so hard to choose.
  I'm held captive
    then weaken and buy one book
      tucked snuggly under my arm.

Store another gem in bookcase
  returning often to gaze
    swoon and moon over the treasures
      like Pavlov's dogs.

Printed words have power
  over me.
    Magic power
      that opens doorways
        to knowledge, adventure, travel
          carry me back or forward
            in time.

But mostly,
  just to enjoy.
    Books are indeed
      my rainy day blessings.

Carousel

When I was three or four,
Daddy took me to the fair.
He thought I'd be thrilled
to ride the merry-go-round.
I wasn't...
        I never saw a carnival.
        It scared me.

Riding a wild, white bronco
with fringed mane of gold and red,
flapping as he galloped and bucked
back and forth up and down,
spinning round and round,
I hang tight to the reins
as it whirled and twirled faster.

Shrunk deep in the saddle trying
to scream " Daddy."
Words froze.
My stomach flopped and churned
like I needed to burp,
        attempting to catch Daddy's attention.

I held my hand up like a traffic officer.
Daddy waved cheerfully back.
I sped like a roaring locomotive
whizzing by the landscape.
Soon losing track of him.

As I caught a glimpse,
  he wore a stupid grin.
    Perhaps imagining himself at the
      Indianapolis 500,
        waving me on with his hat
          like a flagman counting laps.

I yanked at my foot to dismount,
  but it jammed in the stirrup.
    Eventually the machine slowed,
      the world stopped spinning,
        Daddy's face came into focus.

The carousel creaked.
  The organ moaned.
    The horse whinnied and wheezed to a stop.
    The nightmare over.
      Daddy lifted me down,
        and carried me off the platform.

Stealing a glance over my shoulder,
  I saw the operator's hand on the throttle.
    I stuck my tongue out.
      He glared back.

Daddy asked how I enjoyed
  my horsy ride, but when I opened my
    mouth to answer,
      I threw-up all over his
        new shirt.

A Penny's Worth

Round, flat circle of value
  moulded, pressed, spit
    onto greedy tongued belt.
      polished copper coins,
        stamped with bushy tailed beavers,
          maple leaf motifs
            profiles of
              George Vl.

Royal trains squashed pennies flat
  into rare souvenirs
    hoarded in tea pots,
      mason jars, red and
        yellow ceramic piggy banks
          raided with knives, slammed
            by hammers and
              traded for desired object.

Shave and haircut two bits,
  coffee a nickel,
    5 pound potato a dime.

Five and Dime Store became
  poor man's paradise.
    one hundred pennies bought
      a comb, 2 yards satin ribbon, tooth brush,
        lily-of-the-valley talc, jar of Bay Rum
          hair tonic.

One or two pennies got you
  two black ball jawbreakers
    ten coloured jelly beans,
      or two chocolate coated
        honeymoons.

Potpourri

Games

There seems
to be a wall
growing
between us
like a thick
hedge
to keep
intruders out.

I bend toward you
like tall grass
swaying in the
breeze
but you turn,
and
dance away.

The sky is
darkening
and
your face
is fading
in the
distant maze.

If I knew
the name
of the game
you're playing
I'd learn
the rules.

Road Rage

Rush hour
walled in by tractor-trailers
and hitting red lights is nerve wracking.
Patience, explodes into anger.

An eighteen wheeler, grinds to a stop.
The driver a three hundred pound hulk flings open his door,
jumps down
charges up to a beige Taurus
wielding a baseball bat, swinging with the power of a Spartan warrior,
smashes the window as the Taurus driver ducks missing the blow.
The trucker's red tee-shirt reads:
"Don't anger a hungry bear.
He bites."

Shouts something like
" buck" or "luck"
shakes his fist points a finger up,
swaggers back to his rig, tugs up his pants,
and climbs into his cab.
Taurus driver sits in shock, stunned.

A witness grabs his cell phone. Punches 911.
Pounds C.K.L.W.
Surprisingly wins tip of the month.
One hundred dollars...
Smacks his lips, vows to treat his friends
to a juicy New York strip steak.
Thankful he hasn't succumbed to "road rage."
Yet.

Volcano

It's so hard to talk to you.
Before I conjure up words.
Before I tell you who I am.
Before I say I deeply care.

My throat muscles tense...
Seems to snap shut
Like prison bars.
Locking me in.

Voice silent
Words stick to the
Roof of my mouth
Like thick globs of peanut-butter.

Emotions unexpressed....
Suppressed or repressed
Will rage and explode
Into volcanic eruptions.

For those of you who read a book from back to front this is for you:

Sweet Violets are for Memories and Promises of Spring

"When winter sheds his dark grey cloak"
and skitters around the corner. We look for signs of spring.
"Violets rush to greet us when spring knocks on the door."
Their deep purple blue faces never cease to reflect hope.
"They bud and bloom in a field of snow."
Violets may appear diffident and frail with spindly stems,
but like the willow tree they are resillent and bend in the wind.
"Violets sprout new life each year"
and "dance like fairies in the snow."

Violets in the Snow

Snow falling all around,
Violets blossom in cold ground.
Reminding us that spring is near.
Days of pleasant memories dear.

As promises of hope abound,
Sweet fragrances are found.
In clusters they bloom and grow,
And dance like fairies in the snow.

Joy (Toohey) Mac Arthur grew up in Kirkland Lake
where she attended Holy Name School and Kirkland
Lake Collegiate & Vocational Institute. In 1952 she
married Richard MacArthur and they have four
children: Darlyn, Christopher, Richard and Timothy

In 1993 Joy earned a degree in English Literature
from the University of Windsor which was a
lifelong dream. Joy and her husband Richard
have travelled to many parts of the world.

Currently she is involved with (W'INK) Writers' Ink
a writer's group in Windsor, Ontario. Joy is a member
of The Writers Club of Windsor and Essex County.
She is also involved in the Live Poet's Society and
has taken numerous enrichment courses at the
Academy for Learning in Retirement, University of Windsor.

Joy's poetry has appeared in "Visions" an anthology,
"Good Times "magazine and was awarded first prize
for poetry (seniors) at the International Freedom Festival.

ISBN 0-9689349-0-0